Grow in Faith

M. Wells 2001

How to Lead a SUNDAY SCHOOL

For Sunday School Superintendents

by Dale E. Griffin

Edited by the Board for Parish Services Staff
Arnold E. Schmidt, Editor

CPH.
SAINT LOUIS

Erlynne A. Bratvogel, Editorial Assistant

Copyright © 1979, 1992 Concordia Publishing House
3558 South Jefferson Avenue, St. Louis, MO 63118-3968
Manufactured in the United States of America

All rights reserved. No part of this publication may be reproduced, stored in a retrieval system, or transmitted, in any form or by any means, electronic, mechanical, photocopying, recording, or otherwise, without the prior written permission of Concordia Publishing House.

2 3 4 5 6 7 8 9 10   JSS   01 00 99 98

Contents

Preface	4
1. You Have a Ministry!	7
2. Organizing the Sunday School	14
3. Staff Development	27
4. Programs, Materials, and Procedures	33
5. Your Ministry in the Congregation	41
6. You and Your Community	48
Resource Materials	55
Appendix A	56
Appendix B	60
Appendix C	63

Preface

How to Lead a Sunday School is one handbook in the series How to Teach. The series contains the following manuals:

- **How to Reach Very Young Children**
  (for early-childhood program leaders), 22-2501
- **How to Teach Preschoolers**
  (for Nursery and Kindergarten teachers), 22-2502
- **How to Teach Grades 1–4**
  (for Primary and Junior teachers), 22-2503
- **How to Teach Grades 5–8**
  (for Preteen and Junior High teachers), 22-2504
- **How to Teach Teens**
  (for youth Bible class leaders), 22-2505
- **How to Teach Adults**
  (for adult Bible class leaders), 22-2506
- **How to Teach Special Students**
  (for special-education class leaders), 22-2508
- **How to Lead a Sunday School**
  (for Sunday school superintendents), 22-2507

These booklets are designed to help teachers and administrators improve the educational ministry of the congregation by

- clarifying the nature of the teaching task, especially the task of communicating the Word in Sunday school, and
- helping teachers know and understand the students they teach so they can communicate with and relate to their students more appropriately.

These guides may be used in two ways:

1. **Departmental study.** Use one chapter per session with the teachers of the levels involved. Ask participants to read the material in advance. During the session discuss the material. Be

sure to allow time to also discuss the questions at the end of each chapter. Teachers from groups of congregations may hold a series of departmental meetings to discuss the material in these guides. This would also provide an excellent opportunity to share other ideas that might benefit your Sunday school.

2. **Individual study.** Before a new person begins teaching, provide a copy of the appropriate guide to read on her/his own. *Also provide a forum to discuss the material and the teaching task.* Talk with the new teacher yourself, or arrange for your pastor or an experienced teacher from that department to help the new teacher learn more about students and the teaching task.

Study by teachers ought to continue beyond the pages of these guides. You can provide professional help regularly by providing subscriptions of *Teachers Interaction* for all your teachers. Various teachers guides also contain suggestions for additional study.

The **Concordia Teacher Education Program** provides additional in-depth courses. Teachers can learn more about the teaching task and about the material they will teach. See the Concordia Publishing House catalog for information about this program or write for a descriptive brochure from *Sunday School Teacher Education Program, Board for Parish Services, 1333 South Kirkwood Road, St. Louis, MO 63122-7295.*

1 You Have a Ministry!

So you administer a Sunday school! Perhaps you are a pastor, a minister of Christian education, a board member, or a Sunday school superintendent. If you are a volunteer, you may have only limited time to give to this position.

Yet you have an important role to fill in your congregation. You have many opportunities for significant service in the church.

In most congregations the Sunday school is the principal agency for Christian education. Help your congregation recognize its importance. And look for ways your leadership can contribute to your Sunday school's effectiveness.

Why Sunday School?

Most Sunday schools exist for two reasons. They nurture the spiritual growth of members of your congregation, and they minister to people in your community. In Baptism all members of your congregation—children, youth, and adults—were baptized into the family of God.

But Baptism is only a beginning. Throughout life God's people grow spiritually. The Holy Spirit leads them to a deeper understanding of their relation to God, to themselves, to the church, and to society. In Sunday school God's people can gather together to

- deepen their understanding of the Word of God, through which the Spirit nurtures Christian faith and life;
- share their faith and help one another grow in Christian knowledge through their discussions of the Word;
- apply the teachings of the Word to their everyday life;
- encourage one another in the Christian faith and life, especially in times of doubt and difficulties;

- gain skills in living the Christian life, such as in the study of Scripture, prayer, witnessing, stewardship, and worship;
- develop such Christian attitudes as love, kindness, patience, understanding, and compassion;
- learn to know people as individuals, and seek to minister personally to one another;
- grow in their understanding of the ministry and mission of the church, and become personally involved in the church's outreach to all people;
- plan and implement ways to invite the unchurched in the community to join this particular fellowship of God's people;
- serve as an agency for assimilating newer members and friends of the congregation into the congregational fellowship;
- identify community needs and plan ways to minister to those who are hurting.

What a great challenge and opportunity you have! Obviously, your Sunday school will be unable to meet all of these opportunities equally well. But it can accomplish much as your congregation seeks to fulfill its ministry and mission.

But What Is Spiritual Growth?

For many people "spiritual growth" is a rather vague idea. Just what is it?

"Spiritual growth" means more than learning how to live morally according to the Ten Commandments.

Sunday school is not a place where we teach children how to be "good" boys and girls. God did not give us the Bible primarily to teach students what kind of life they are to follow or avoid. Nor does He intend that we make moral heroes out of certain Bible characters and villains out of others. Such an emphasis would miss the message of grace that God offers in His Word.

That approach to the Bible assumes that people in themselves have the power to become good and acceptable to God. But this is not the message God gives in the Scriptures.

Law

The Bible first of all teaches us that we must be realistic in our understanding of ourselves and of the human situation. Through His Law, such as in the Ten Commandments, God teaches us what He expects of us—an expectation that no human being can attain.

Thus, the Law reveals our sinful nature and our need for God to be gracious and forgiving toward us.

The Law teaches us how we are to be, and what we are to do or not to do. Thereby the Law emphasizes our hopeless, helpless situation before God. Of ourselves we are powerless to remedy this situation.

Thus, we are not free to live as we please. God's Law points out that we are morally responsible to a just God. We are accountable to Him for how we live out our days in His world; we live under His judgment. Of course, we cannot attain perfection. On our own we would be condemned to an eternity apart from God, the giver of all life. In this sense the Law drives us to despair.

Gospel

But the Bible has a good word for us. We know that we daily sin and deserve God's wrath. In His infinite love toward us, God took our guilt upon Himself. He became human in the person of Jesus and fulfilled His own demands. Jesus led the perfect life in our stead.

Moreover, Jesus assumed the burden of our sinfulness. He suffered the very pangs of hell on the cross in the place of us all. In Jesus, God satisfied the justice our sin required. To establish His victory over sin and death, Jesus rose again. He lives in our hearts now and in the world to come.

We must make the Gospel of Jesus Christ the center of our Sunday school ministry. Jesus *has* delivered us from sin. In Him we enjoy life with God both here on earth and in heaven.

Law and Gospel

Every Sunday school lesson should contain a clear message of Law and Gospel. Students must recognize that on their own they are helpless, sinful beings. But, even though they do not deserve it, God deals with them in grace. Because of this underserved love He sent Jesus to be our Savior.

For example, we do not teach that God accepted Abraham because he was a good man. On the contrary, Abraham was a very sinful man. But God in His grace chose Abraham to be His servant and the father of His people. God promised Abraham that He would send a Savior. The Old Testament people of God trusted in His gracious promises, and thereby they were saved.

God's grace comes to us, too. Through the work of His Spirit we now are His people.

But what does it mean to live as God's people today? In our Sunday school lessons we seek to help people grow, by the power of the Holy Spirit, in their relationship with their gracious God. We also desire that students mature as Christian persons in their relationships with their family, their church, and their world.

Power for Growth

How can your Sunday school be effective? Among other things you will need a good staff. Look for teachers who

- model the Christian faith and life in their own lives;
- worship and participate in Bible study regularly;
- understand and love the students they teach;
- demonstrate some understanding of how people learn;
- use good teaching techniques and methods.

God uses people to do His work. We urge you to select the best teachers in your congregation for your Sunday school ministry.

But you need more than competent teachers. Those teachers need the power God provides. It is He who motivates and enables both teachers and students to believe and to live as His people.

The real power for spiritual growth comes from the Holy Spirit. He works through the Word your teachers share. Be sure, therefore, to build your Sunday school program on the Bible as its ultimate basis.

As indicated earlier, the message of the Bible is Law and Gospel. Both center in Jesus Christ. The Law shows our need for the salvation provided in Jesus. The Gospel reveals what God in Christ has done, and continues to do, for eternal salvation.

We can teach the Bible in many different ways.

1. **We can teach basic Bible narratives and apply their meanings to the students' lives.** For this we may use the words of the Bible or recast them into simpler language according to the maturity level of the students being taught.

2. **Especially for youth and adults we can study a specific book of the Bible.** We then take into account

    - the historical setting of the book;
    - the purpose of the writer;
    - the needs or problems being addressed;
    - what the writer has to say to specific people living in a particular situation;

- what all of this means for our Christian faith and life in today's setting.

3. **We can select a theme and review what the entire Bible has to say about it.** The Catechism is organized according to this method.

   At times students, particularly youth and adults, may wish to study other themes of current interest. For example, youth may study what the Scriptures have to say about marriage and the family. In such a study the biblical teaching can be related easily to contemporary thought and trends.

4. **We can use symbols—visible signs of the invisible realities—to teach Bible truths.** The early church often used the cross to draw attention to Jesus' work of salvation for us. It used the fish to represent Jesus and those who in faith identified with Him. Today we use many symbolic forms to communicate scriptural truths—art, drama, films, videotapes, colors, and other media.

Regardless of the methods or forms of Bible study we use, we must depend upon the work of the Holy Spirit. It is He who works through scriptural words and concepts to achieve His purposes.

Your Role

Your congregation has called you to an important position of leadership. You are responsible to the entire congregation, but you probably will work with a board of Christian education. This board can help you fulfill such duties as

- forming statements of purpose (mission statement) and general policies for the Sunday school;
- creating job descriptions for all Sunday school staff persons;
- selecting Sunday school teachers and staff;
- preparing teachers and staff for their service (teachers' meetings);
- securing adequate financial support;
- obtaining curriculum materials;
- providing the Sunday school with sufficient equipment and space;
- planning a systematic program of visitation with parents, students (both enrollees and prospects), visitors, absentees, and others;
- developing effective publicity within both the congregation and the community;

- administering a comprehensive outreach ministry within the local community;
- offering mission-education programs and projects;
- cultivating a disciplined climate for learning and fellowship;
- supporting and encouraging all Sunday school teachers and staff persons in their ministry;
- reporting Sunday school activities and progress regularly to the congregation.

Be sure to work closely with your pastor and, if you have one, your director of Christian education (DCE). The pastor is responsible for the spiritual well-being and growth of all members of the congregation, including the Sunday school and its program. Plan to discuss your plans and problems with him. If his schedule permits—at least on occasion—encourage him to visit Sunday school classes and to offer helpful suggestions. Also invite him to attend staff meetings. Keep him abreast of the Sunday school program and ask him to provide guidance.

A DCE has been trained to provide professional knowledge in all aspects of your work as superintendent. He or she can help you identify potential staff members, develop the curriculum and program, train teachers, and improve various aspects of the Sunday school ministry.

Your teaching staff is the heart of the Sunday school. Work with your board of education, pastor, and DCE to select new teachers. Then provide adequate training for them, assist them in discipline situations, help them plan a complete program, and in other ways support the teachers in their ministry.

Your board of education can also help you assemble a support staff to assist you in your administrative activities. You need not do everything yourself. Your congregation gives you the responsibility to see that the Sunday school program is alive and vibrant. To accomplish this, work closely with all members of the support staff so that they are enabled to function with joy.

Also work to cultivate the friendship of the Sunday school students. Look for ways to make it possible for you to

- greet students as they arrive;
- participate in worship assemblies;
- visit study groups;
- participate in fellowship events;
- cultivate in a variety of settings your acquaintance with individual members of the Sunday school;

- learn to know all parents of students;
- interpret your Sunday school program to parents and cultivate their goodwill.

Administration can strongly influence the success of a Sunday school program. Your position is very important. With a spirit of consecration look to the Holy Spirit for help. He will give you the power to do your work well!

Questions for Discussion

1. What led you to become a Sunday school leader? In what ways will your motives contribute to the effectiveness of your Sunday school?

2. In your opinion, what purposes does your congregation have for its Sunday school?

3. Does your congregation have an adequate understanding of the Sunday school's purposes? If not, what can you do to help the congregation develop this understanding?

4. How would you describe the morale of the teachers and students in your Sunday school? Do you believe they have a clear understanding of the Sunday school's purposes? What can you do to improve the morale of your Sunday school?

5. Inasmuch as the effectiveness of your Sunday school depends on the work of the Holy Spirit, why is it important to select teachers with adequate teaching skills? What importance would you attach to a teacher's spiritual gifts?

6. Why are many adults, youth, and children seemingly untouched by God's Spirit in their church school?

2 Organizing the Sunday School

God gave people the ability to think and plan. Clearly defined tasks and goals help them function effectively. Ideally, they also understand the way their activity is organized. Leaders of a congregation must identify the God-given talents of the people, then organize them for ministry. Such information and organization can contribute to effective ministry. You are a key person in overseeing this ministry in your Sunday school.

What Are You Trying to Do?

Take special action at the beginning of each Sunday school year. Gather a group of representative people. Work through your understanding of the purposes of your school. Establish clear goals for the coming year. This group may include members of the Sunday school staff, members of the board of education, parents, and others interested in the Sunday school program.

1. **First brainstorm ideas of your Sunday school's purpose.** You might organize these ideas into a statement of purpose, a philosophy, or a mission statement. Following are two sample mission statements:

   "The purpose of Peace Lutheran Sunday School is, as Christ commanded His church, to make disciples of all nations through the nurture of those within the congregation and through the outreach to those who don't yet know Jesus as Savior" (Courtesy, Peace Lutheran Church, Lemay, MO).

   "To proclaim the Gospel of Jesus Christ and to demonstrate God's love to one another, the community, and the world" (Courtesy, Glendale Lutheran Church, Glendale, MO).

2. **Next, formulate goals and objectives.** Objectives tend to be more specific than goals. Seek objectives that
   - include changes of behavior in understanding, attitudes, behaviors, and/or skills;
   - are stated in behavioral terms (e.g., the students may be able to recite the Lord's Prayer);
   - are attainable;
   - are measurable (e.g., you can ascertain whether or not a student can recite the Lord's Prayer).

Formulate enough objectives to be challenging, but not so many that you are overwhelmed.

Assess the progress during the year, possibly quarterly. Which objectives are you obtaining? What progress have you made since your last assessment?

Also plan a year-end evaluation. How well has your Sunday school met its goals and objectives? Which strategies are working well, and which need to be improved? What good things need to be continued? What changes should be made? This evaluation will give your group a basis on which to plan for the following year.

Class Organization

Following is a common organizational pattern. Your curricular materials may suggest some variations.

1. **Nursery or cradle roll.** Plan to use this program for all baptized infants and their parents. Less than 60 percent of children baptized in our churches later become involved in the Sunday school. Look for nursery-roll materials that will support this important ministry.
2. **Two-year-olds and their parents.** Parents are the primary teachers of young children. If possible, provide a program for parents and 2's. Through this program you can assist parents during this vital period of their child's life. This program can also serve as a transition into a program (class) in which parents are not present. A program for two-year-olds can become a significant first step in involving young children in formal Christian education experiences.
3. **Nursery and Kindergarten department.** Provide an appropriate setting for children three to six years old.
4. **A Primary and Junior department** for students in grades 1–4. Some congregations group primary classes (grades 1–2)

with the Nursery and Kindergarten department, and combine grades 3–4 with grades 5–6.

5. **A Preteen and Junior High department** for grades 5–8. Grades 7–8 may form a separate department, and grades 5–6 may be grouped with grades 3–4.
6. **The high school or youth department.** This may be divided into classes for each of the four high school grades. Or you may place grades 9–10 in one class and grades 11–12 in another. Some congregations group classes for high school students according to topics being offered.
7. **An adult department** for all adults. Form study groups according to interests of potential participants.

These classes may be combined into departments for assembly and administrative purposes. The number of departments will depend largely on the number of students enrolled and the assembly space available. Your local situation will help you determine your organization.

Do not neglect persons with learning disabilities. Identify these people in your congregation and community and provide Christian education experiences for them. Some congregations have separate groups for these people and use the special-education materials provided through Concordia Publishing House. Others place these people in the regular classes. In these instances, be sure to integrate students with learning disabilities into the group. Treat them with respect and kindness, and involve them in the learning activities in appropriate ways.

The Teaching Staff

Later we will discuss teacher selection and training. We suggest at least one teacher for every ten students, plus teacher helpers as needed. Provide two teachers for early-childhood groups. If one small child requires attention, another adult is available to care for the other children.

You have only a limited time for Christian education through the Sunday school. Do all you can to keep classes small for efficient learning and group interaction.

If possible, even for classes of older students, provide two teachers for each class. These two can prepare and present the lesson together. If one is absent, the other can teach without breaking the continuity.

If you cannot enlist two teachers, attempt to secure helpers. High school students often make excellent helpers. At the same time they are developing skills to become Sunday school teachers themselves later in life.

If you have only one teacher per class, you will need a reservoir of substitute teachers. Be sure to formulate and carry through a clear procedure for the use of substitutes. If teachers need to be absent, clarify whom they should notify. You might have them contact a substitute directly. Or they could notify you or their department leader. Be sure substitutes always have sufficient time for preparation.

In addition to securing teachers, plan ways to orient them to their tasks, arrange in-service training for them, and involve them in the decision-making processes of the Sunday school. Such involvement can help teacher morale and contribute to a pleasing atmosphere for your entire Sunday school ministry.

The Sunday School Program

A crucial element of the Sunday school program is curriculum development and the selection of materials. Ask your pastor, DCE, and board of education to help you in this vital undertaking.

Plan ways to avoid duplication and provide ordered progression. For preconfirmation children be sure to correlate the Sunday school program with that of the weekday school, Christian day school, and vacation Bible school.

Consider securing all materials from one source. In this way the learning experiences on a given grade level are built on those in lower grades.

Strongly consider using the educational materials produced by your own denomination. They will be in harmony with the goals, teachings, and policies of that Christian fellowship of which you are a part.

Stimulate interest and participation by employing a variety of materials and teaching techniques. Examine the suggestions for audiovisual resources as well as printed matter in the Sunday morning program. Consider equipment for videocassettes, audiocassettes, and compact disks. Many teachers will also appreciate an overhead projector, a chalkboard, or a marker board for erasable markers.

Judicious, purposeful use of audiovisual materials can significantly contribute to the Sunday school learning experience.

Take a careful look at the Sunday morning session itself. Help your staff organize it for interest, variety, and effectiveness.

Plan every detail of the program. Leave nothing to chance. For example, do the following yourself or arrange for someone else to do them:

1. Open the building and check on classroom arrangements, heating or cooling, ventilation, and lighting.
2. Welcome students and visitors and direct them to their places.
3. Develop a program of activities for those who arrive before classes begin.
4. Enroll new members and get acquainted with them.
5. Arrange responsibilities for group openings when several classes meet together for opening worship. Correlate the worship activities with the lesson for the day. Some educational experiences might take place during this assembly period.
6. Arrange the handling of the offering and the keeping of records.
7. Arrange for necessary announcements and distribution of materials.
8. Note the absentees and new students; arrange for a follow-up.
9. Deal with problems noted by staff members.
10. Check teacher or class arrangements and adjust if necessary (e.g., divide a class with too many students).
11. Encourage teachers and students to attend church worship and to participate in other Sunday school and congregational events.
12. After sessions end, check on lights, heat, etc., and close the building.

Many Sunday schools' students participate in special worship services. Most often these occur in connection with Rally Day and Christmas. Services and pageants might also be offered for such times as Reformation Sunday, Thanksgiving Day, Lent, and Easter. You will need to help organize, plan, and present these children's services.

Social events can help students and teachers develop a sense of belonging and fellowship. Consider parties on Reformation Day, Christmas, Easter, or another time of the year. Perhaps you can plan picnics, retreats, swim parties, and other outdoor events during the warmer months. Or consider sledding, ice skating, and similar activities during winter months in colder states.

Well-conducted social events can contribute much to Sunday school morale.

The Physical Plant

Make your congregation aware of the need for adequate and appropriate space for the Sunday school. Make this a priority of a building or remodeling program.

Periodically assess the space available and plan for the best possible use of this space for assemblies and classes. Don't forget the need for ample storage space and for Sunday school administration.

Also give attention to the care of property. Work with the appropriate board in your congregation to be sure that the Sunday school area is clean and that furniture is in good repair.

Check the property for safety hazards. Notify the trustees if heating, cooling, ventilation, or lighting systems need attention. Make sure the church carries adequate insurance for the protection of the property and people.

Be alert to equipment needs. Periodically check the condition of Sunday school furnishings and equipment. Be sure they are in good condition and are adequate for instructional needs. The following guide may be helpful:

NURSERY

Staff
Two adults for 8–10 children, plus one for each additional 5–6 children

Space
25 to 40 sq. ft. per child

Equipment
10" chairs
Table 10" higher than chairs
Small tea table
Center table for art and beauty
Bible or Bible story book
Audiocassette player
Record player
Simple puzzles
Large blocks
Picture books
40" easels
Suitable toys

Space for coats/jackets, etc.
Storage and display space
Warm floor safe for children's play
Materials such as paper, large crayons, clay
Sand table
Videotape player and monitor
Flannelgraph equipment

KINDERGARTEN

Staff
At least 2 adults for every 12–14 children, plus one for each additional 5 or 6 children

Space
25 to 30 sq. ft. per child

Equipment
12" chairs
Tables 10" higher than chairs
Center table for art and beauty
Small tea table
Housekeeping toys
Blocks
Easels
Audiocassette player
Videotape player and monitor
Record player
Work materials such as paper, crayons, scissors, clay
Flannelgraph equipment
Sand table
Storage and display space
Space for coats/jackets, etc.
Warm floor safe for play
Bible or Bible story books
Other appropriate books
Chalkboard or marker board
Corkboard

ELEMENTARY GRADES

Staff
One adult for every 5–8 students.

With larger classes, a number of adults can engage in team teaching.

Space
20 to 30 sq. ft. per student

Equipment
14" and 16" chairs
Table 10" higher than chairs
Tables for worship and interest centers
Record player
Audiocassette player
Videotape player and monitor
Bibles and Bible story books
Resource books
Flannelgraph for lower grades
Rhythm instruments for lower grades
Hymnals or songbooks
Work materials as for writing
Construction and drawing paper
Crayons or felt pens, scissors, newsprint, paints, brushes
Storage and display space
Chalkboard or marker board
Maps
Corkboard
Easels
Overhead projector for upper grades
Space for coats/jackets, etc.

YOUTH

Staff
One teacher for every 5–7 students.
Teaching teams of about 2 teachers to every 10–14 students desirable.

Space
12 to 18 sq. ft. per person

Equipment
15" to 16" chairs
Tables 10" higher than chairs
Tables for worship and interest centers

Record player
Audiocassette player
Videocassette player and monitor
Bibles
Hymnals and songbooks
Reference and resource books
Materials such as marking pens, newsprint, pencils, paper
Storage and display space
Chalkboard or marker board
Corkboard
Maps
Easels
Overhead projector

ADULTS

Staff
Staffing determined by number and type of classes.

Space
12 to 18 sq. ft. per person

Equipment
16" chairs
Tables 10" higher than chairs
Record player
Audiocassette player
Videocassette player and monitor
Bibles
Hymnals
Reference and resource books
Maps
Chalkboard or marker board
Corkboard
Materials such as pencils, paper, newsprint, and marking pens
Storage space
Easels
Overhead projector

The individual Sunday school may adapt these suggestions to its own situation.

Public Relations

Plan ways to interpret and publicize your school. Look for ways to reach both your congregation and your community. Some suggestions follow. We hope they will also stimulate you to think of other ideas.

In your congregation you might

- publish a Sunday school newsletter to be sent to Sunday school students and their parents (and to the other members of the congregation if budget permits);
- use bulletin boards in strategic places to post the work of students and to publicize Sunday school events;
- recognize birthdays, Baptism anniversaries, and other special events in the lives of individual students and teachers;
- maintain a thorough visitation or contact ministry to absentees and visitors;
- publicize the Sunday school at every opportunity in church publications;
- talk up the Sunday school in congregational meetings;
- encourage the pastor and other significant persons in the congregation to emphasize the Sunday school and its ministry.

In your community you might

- make generous use of community newspapers for news items and paid advertisements;
- advertise public events of your Sunday school by placing posters in store windows and other public places;
- publicize your Sunday school through radio spot announcements;
- develop programs with children for your local radio or TV station;
- become active in community organizations, especially those involving parents. (Your presence and your interest in community affairs and children are in themselves good advertisements for your Sunday school ministry.)

Many businesses will more likely accept posters made by students than posters made by adults. Do not insist on placing a poster in a store if the store manager or owner is reluctant.

Support Staff

You and your teachers already have a big job. You need other people to support your ministry. Below we suggest officers who might support you and your teachers.

Obviously, smaller congregations will not require so many support officers. The functions can be distributed among several people according to local circumstances.

1. **Assistant superintendent.** This person helps carry out the regular activities of the superintendent and takes over when the superintendent is absent. After serving a term as assistant, this person could succeed the current superintendent.
2. **Recording and corresponding secretary.** This person keeps records and takes care of correspondence.
3. **Visitation secretary.** This officer notes the names of absentees and visitors and arranges for these people to be contacted or visited whenever appropriate.
4. **Curriculum secretary.** This person orders curriculum materials and distributes them to classes. This person may also serve as the audiovisual resource director.
5. **Audiovisual resource director.** This person is responsible for the acquisition, care, and use of all audiovisual equipment. He or she orders videotapes, films, audiotapes, and other resources; stores them for future use; and keeps an index of all audiovisual holdings. This person trains teachers and others in the proper use of the AV equipment.
6. **Nursery-roll coordinator.** This important person enrolls in the nursery roll every infant baptized in the church and administers a ministry to these children and their parents until the children are enrolled in a Sunday morning class. In addition to sending periodic mailings, this person arranges for frequent visits to be made in the homes of nursery-roll children. Consider using *Beginnings*, the Concordia nursery-roll packet for this ministry.
7. **Treasurer.** Many congregations include Sunday school finances in their budget operation. Sunday schools in other congregations need a treasurer to handle the Sunday school offerings, keep financial records, and disburse funds.
8. **Director of teacher education.** Use a gifted individual, such as a professionally educated teacher, to prepare volunteer teachers for their ministry. Provide new teachers with an orientation course to help them better understand the students they are to teach. Also give instruction in teaching methods and techniques and introduce teachers to the materials they will use.

The director of teacher education might also arrange courses in psychology, education theory, and teaching methods for all teachers. (Usually the pastor is the most qualified to instruct teachers in the Bible and in theology.) If your congregation has a DCE, this person may fulfill the functions of this position.

9. **Activities and assimilation director.** Social and athletic events can enhance your Sunday school program. They provide opportunities for strengthening the bonds of fellowship among the members of the congregation as well as for friends and newer members. But "what is everybody's business is nobody's business." Therefore you may enlist a specific person to develop this aspect of the school's ministry to members and friends.

10. **Music director and staff.** Make music an important part of Sunday school life. Select a person to oversee the entire music program. Involve others with specific musical talents in the various aspects of this program.

    This director might develop a staff of choir directors, pianists, song leaders, and instrumentalists for the Sunday school's music program. You may even develop a small orchestra to give students the opportunity to use their talents in the church.

11. **Outreach director.** A Sunday school ought to have two purposes—nurture of the congregation's members and outreach to the unchurched in the community. Select an individual to develop and administer a program of outreach for the Sunday school. This director would also work closely with the congregation's board for outreach.

12. **Mission education director.** This person will identify ways for students to develop a sense of responsibility for the evangelization of the whole world. Students may learn about mission activities of their church body. If possible, give them an opportunity to participate in mission activities.

Select suggestions from this chapter to help you develop a vibrant, dynamic school ministry. Then pray for the Holy Spirit's blessing and carefully plan the ways you organize and implement the suggestions.

Questions for Discussion

1. What goals does your Sunday school have? What can you do to publicize those goals—or develop them, if you have none?

2. What plans does your Sunday school have for the next 12 months? What events and projects might be feasible?

3. What is the organizational pattern of your Sunday school? Is it working? How might it be improved?

4. Does your Sunday school have an inventory of all resources and equipment? If not, what might you do to develop a complete inventory?

5. What kind of public-relations program on behalf of your Sunday school do you offer your congregation and community? What might you do to improve it?

6. What support officers does your Sunday school have? What functions are not being provided for? What might be done to reorganize the support staff to make it more helpful?

3 Staff Development

Teaching is the heart of the Sunday school program. Teachers teach both by word and example. Therefore you must select them with care. Also provide opportunities for them to grow in their personal Christian faith and life as well as in their teaching skills.

The Teacher's Role

First of all, teachers are to be examples of Christian life and witness and, second, communicators. They are to share with their students what it means to be Christian and how to live as children of God in this world of wickedness and unbelief.

Teachers themselves need to grow in their understanding of the faith and in their Christian life in order to better share the faith.

Teachers serve in a "shepherd" role. This role demands genuine interest in their students as individuals. God's "shepherds" guide their students in their personal development as believing children of God. At times teachers will have opportunity to counsel individual students about their problems and questions. Therefore seek teachers with Christian maturity.

Teachers facilitate discussion. They give all members of the study group the opportunity and privilege to share their faith, and to describe what Christian faith can mean for everyday life.

A teacher is also a model. We all learn from observing other people and how they function. Some people will enter a specific career because they admire a person in that chosen occupation.

Students observe the Christian attitudes and lifestyle of Sunday school teachers. Students who respect their teachers will likely seek to emulate their beliefs and lifestyle.

Enlisting New Teachers

Research has indicated that teacher selection is more significant than teacher training. The Holy Spirit has chosen not to give the gift of teaching to everyone. Select teachers with great care.

Teaching is an art as well as a science; many intangible factors go into the making of a good teacher. Look for characteristics like these in the prospective teachers.

1. **They are committed Christians.** Students detect "phonies" quickly. Teachers cannot communicate effectively that which they do not believe.
2. **They are regular in their church attendance and in Bible study.** They are willing to grow in their understanding of the Bible, Christian doctrine, and their church. Most volunteer teachers do not possess the knowledge they would like to have. But "good" teachers want to grow.
3. **They understand and love the people they will teach.** Some teachers do better with one age level than with another. Do all you can to match teachers and students.
4. **They have a positive attitude toward the Christian faith and their church.** Teachers who take potshots at Christianity or their church can do great harm.
5. **They sincerely appreciate the significance of Sunday school ministry and have a high regard for its work.**
6. **They are willing to visit the homes of their students.** Visits can help teachers

   - understand the students they teach and their home environment;
   - cultivate the support of the parents;
   - demonstrate their genuine love and concern for their students and their parents;
   - identify student needs;
   - encourage students and their parents to be faithful in Sunday school and church participation and in leading a Christian life;
   - minister in whatever ways they discover through such visits.

Now ask: *How many teachers do we need?* Many teachers want freedom to plan different weekend activities occasionally. Therefore try to enlist two teachers for each study group. Or provide a strong group of substitutes.

Don't wait until you have a severe shortage of teachers before beginning an enlistment program. Also, do not merely insert a general invitation in church publications in the hope that sufficient volunteers will step forward. This procedure does little for the strength of your Sunday school or for teacher morale.

There is a better way.

1. Go through your congregation's membership list and identify those people whom you feel have the ability to teach.
2. Submit your list of prospective teachers to your board of education. Plan how you will extend an invitation to those potential Sunday school workers.
3. Identify the person who will extend the invitation. People react differently to different persons. Some would react most favorably to your invitation. Others may be friends with an individual member of the board and would respond more favorably to that person. Still others may welcome an invitation from your pastor.
4. Telephone potential teachers and arrange for an interview in their home. You may want to invite two people in this visit.
5. During the visit explain the needs of the Sunday school, the importance of the Sunday school teacher, and the reasons why that person was selected. Provide a brief position description.
6. Help new teachers become oriented to Sunday school teaching. They might work with an experienced teacher for a few weeks before assuming their own class.
7. Also consider a brief orientation course to help new teachers develop a better understanding of the persons they will teach, effective teaching methods, and the materials to be used. Concordia Publishing House offers several resources for such courses.
8. Even when you have no immediate need for new teachers, identify persons who may serve as teachers in the future. Especially look at the gifts of those who have just joined your congregation.

Keep the Good Teachers You Have

It is easy to take teachers for granted—particularly those who have served faithfully for many years. You cannot picture the Sunday school without these persons.

Teachers are a gift of God. Be sure to recognize and encourage them. You can do much to establish and maintain a willing, happy staff.

Regularly observe the work of your teachers. Praise them for whatever good they do. When you make a suggestion for improvement, be sure to add words of encouragement for the work they are doing.

Let your teachers know you are interested in them and that you appreciate their service.

Be sensitive to the needs of your teachers, and give them the help they desire. Encourage them when they want to try some new approaches or methods. Demonstrate your appreciation for new ideas they offer, even when the ideas may not be feasible. Help them obtain teaching materials and equipment they need. Let your demeanor during the Sunday morning session and the teachers' meetings reflect your high regard for your Sunday school teachers and your willingness to support them.

Occasionally recognize your teachers in special ways. Some congregations provide annual recognition banquets or dinners. You might recognize the work of individual classes through bulletin board displays or church publications.

In his sermons on Rally Day and at other times the pastor might express the congregation's appreciation for the ministry of Sunday school teachers.

Some congregations give their Sunday school teachers helpful books. One congregation gave each teacher $100 worth of reference and resource books just to express its appreciation and to provide teachers with tools for teaching.

Staff Formation and Support

Ideally, Sunday school teachers will display a willingness to grow. Plan teachers' meetings that provide help for Sunday's lesson.

Also offer opportunities for teachers to grow in their overall understanding of the Bible and biblical doctrine, in skills in teaching methods and techniques, in the use of audiovisual equipment, in knowing their students, and in some knowledge of the history of the church.

Allow time at meetings for teachers to discuss their problems, to plan new programs, and to make those decisions that affect their Sunday school ministry.

Teachers meetings may serve several purposes and be organized in various ways.

- **Orientation meetings** help new teachers gain a better understanding of people, teaching methods, curriculum materials, and teaching resources.

- **Lesson preparation meetings** can help teachers plan each week's lessons. The entire staff can meet together if you use a uniform Sunday school series. Some staffs prefer meetings of age-level departments (e.g., nursery-kindergarten; grades 1–4; grades 5–8; and youth/adult). Your local situation will suggest the kinds of lesson preparation meetings best for you.
- **Youth-ministry meetings** can help leaders plan cooperative work. Involve youth counselors and leaders of study groups. Those involved can discuss Sunday morning session preparation as well as all other aspects of the congregational youth program.
- **Adult-education meetings** can help leaders plan an overall comprehensive adult education program both for Sunday mornings and for other times during the week. This group might plan and administer the adult education offerings and programs. Design as many opportunities that encourage as many adults as possible to enroll in at least one group.
- **"Business" meetings of the entire Sunday school staff** enable you to set policies, resolve difficulties, develop and evaluate objectives, and plan the overall Sunday school program.
- **Professional growth meetings** provide opportunities for extended study of the Bible and pertinent topics or issues in education.
- **The Concordia Sunday School Teacher Education Program** offers a variety of courses for this purpose. Most are designed for six or eight sessions. Your pastor, director of Christian education, or other competent persons may develop supplemental courses for the in-service training of teachers.
- **Extended courses** may be held one night a week for a period of weeks. Some parishes hold weekend retreats or all-day Saturday meetings once or twice a year for intensive study.
- **Area workshops** enable teachers from different settings to come together to share ideas. At these workshops a group of congregations can invite experts in various areas of Christian education to serve as leaders.
- **Sunday school associations** provide another forum for cooperative learning. The congregations in a circuit or area may form Sunday school associations. Groups of congregations can also plan cooperative projects. Associations might plan half-day or evening meetings once or twice a year.

- **Regional or district meetings** usually offer several workshops. Teachers may receive help in areas of special interest or need.
- **National Sunday school conventions** provide an even greater variety of teacher-growth opportunities.
- ***Teachers Interaction,*** a national magazine available from Concordia Publishing House can foster teacher growth. This periodical offers much pertinent material for your teachers and provides many resources for your training meetings. We recommend that you order a personal subscription for every staff member.

Encourage teachers to study also at home. Study of the Bible itself is important for every Sunday school worker. Reference books and publications dealing with the Bible and its teachings are also valuable resources for the teacher's home study. Many congregations provide their teachers with such study materials.

Teachers are your Sunday school's backbone. Treat them with care!

Questions for Discussion

1. What qualities do you look for in potential teachers?

2. What procedures do you use to enlist new teachers? How might these procedures be improved?

3. What kind of training do you think new teachers should have?

4. Outline an in-service training program for your teachers for the next year. As you do so, keep in mind the needs of the teachers and the needs of your school.

5. What does your congregation do to recognize and express appreciation for its Sunday school staff members? What else might you do?

6. In what ways can you as a Sunday school leader contribute toward an even higher level of morale among your teachers?

4 Programs Materials and Procedures

Your Sunday school exists primarily for the spiritual development of the members of your congregation and the unchurched people in your community.

In your school a number of forces contribute to the students' growth.

1. The Spirit of God Himself works through the Word to accomplish His gracious purposes. At times you share that Word in conversation, music, and other ways of presenting the "old, old story of Jesus and His love."
2. Students come from a variety of backgrounds. These will influence the way Sunday school experiences affect them.
3. Students learn from Sunday school teachers, staff members, and other adults what it means to be a child of God. We all are teaching through our words, attitudes, and behavior.
4. Student families are perhaps the most influential teachers. Look for way to cooperate with the families and involve them in the church's educational ministry.
5. Students teach one another through discussion and through the ways they interact among one another.
6. The setting and equipment can influence the students. For example, if the congregation expends much care and money to have pleasant facilities and adequate equipment, students gain the impression that Sunday school must be important.
7. Sunday school programs, materials, and procedures influence students' growth in the faith. For instance, if a note of joy permeates the Sunday school and teachers are enthusiastic about their ministry, students learn that Christianity is a religion of joy and hope.

Some materials, however, convey the impression that Christianity is little more than a moral system and that any religion teaching good morals is as good as Christianity. Therefore it is important to examine materials carefully. Use those that maintain the proper distinction between Law and Gospel as they present the teachings of the Bible and that place Jesus Christ in the center.

What Is the "Curriculum"?

Curriculum means more than the courses of study and the study materials, although these are important elements. In a wide sense, the curriculum includes all the experiences of life through which the learner develops understandings, attitudes, skills, and behavior patterns. In a narrow sense, the curriculum refers to the planned experiences of the learner.

When we think of the curriculum in the narrow sense, we refer to what happens to people in a given Sunday school throughout the year. Learners in the Sunday school are to be confronted with the Word of the Gospel in all they do. This includes conversation, worship, mission and stewardship education, Bible reading and study, preparation for special observance, social events, lesson discussions and activities, and presession activities.

Everything that happens in the Sunday school is an important part of the curriculum. It will either nurture Christian faith and life or harm such faith.

Therefore teachers need to think about much more than their lesson presentations. They must consider all facets of the Sunday school program and activities, as well as the lives of their students.

The Lesson Materials

Concordia Publishing House offers a wide variety of materials for all levels of your Sunday school.

- **A Nursery (Cradle) Roll packet.** This can assist your ministry with parents of children from birth to age 3. This packet provides new parents with suggestions and resources to aid them with their child's spiritual growth. It supplies congregations with materials they can use in their outreach to all parents of small children—in the congregation and beyond.
- **Materials for two-year-olds and their parents.** These courses help teachers and parents work together to bring the good news of Jesus to young children. This setting also enables

children to move gradually from the security of their parents to a less frightening age 3 experience without parents present.
- **Nursery and Kindergarten materials.** These include teachers guides, teachers packets, packets of lesson and activity material, *Happy Times* magazine, puppets, and other helpful resources.
- **Materials for grades 1–8.** These are group-graded: Primary (grades 1–2), Junior (grades 3–4), Preteen (grades 5–6), and Junior High (grades 7–8).

  Features of this series are a comprehensive three-year cycle of Bible narratives; lessons for Christmas, Easter, and Pentecost as they occur each year; uniform lessons and worship themes on all four levels; and a Bible commentary to unify teacher training. Study leaflets or guides, activity packets, teachers guides, *My Devotions,* take-home items, and other resources are available.
- **Youth and adult courses.** Because high school youth and adults like to have many options for their study program, Concordia Publishing House offers approximately 100 courses to provide a rich menu from which to choose. You may get a complete listing of available courses from Concordia Publishing House, 3558 South Jefferson Avenue, Saint Louis, MO 63118.
- **Special-education materials.** These are designed to enable volunteer teachers to bring God's good news to persons with various learning disabilities.
- **Take-home magazines and story papers.** These help extend the Sunday lesson through the week. See Concordia Publishing House's curriculum order form for a complete list of titles.
- *Teachers Interaction.* Teachers can use this periodical individually or in teacher-training groups.
- **The Concordia Teacher Education series.** You can use these courses about the Bible, Christian doctrine, and teaching methods for the in-service training of your teachers. If possible, offer your staff at least one or two courses each year.

Concordia Publishing House offers other resources to complement your curricular materials. These include videocassette tapes, audiocassette tapes, and storybooks. Concordia also provides record forms, attendance plans, and other resources for your work as a Sunday school administrator.

For your assistance as you seek to reach out into your community, Concordia provides the *Come, Grow with Us* program. For a complete catalog, see your pastor or request a catalog from Concordia Publishing House.

What Kind of Materials Ought We Use?

Sunday school materials must be sound scripturally, theologically, and educationally. Following are some criteria that might help you evaluate materials.

Objectives are
- theologically and educationally sound;
- supportive of your congregation's objectives for your Sunday school;
- consistent with your congregation's views of its ministry;
- clearly stated and followed throughout the material.

The **content**
- is Christ-centered;
- is Bible-based;
- maintains the proper distinction between Law and Gospel;
- demonstrates concern for changes in attitudes and actions and for the development of Christian understanding and skills;
- is related to the maturity level, needs, and experiences of students at each age level;
- helps people live the Christian faith in their everyday life;
- uses a style and vocabulary understandable and suitable to each age level;
- maintains the dignity of every human being in every culture.

The content of the **teachers guide**
- helps teachers develop a mature understanding of the Bible and of Christian doctrine;
- provides adequate resources and helps;
- views the teacher as a guide, enabler, and co-learner in the teaching-learning process;
- stimulates leaders to do creative thinking and planning.

The **teaching methods** used in the materials
- reflect the best principles of how people learn;
- involve students actively in the teaching/learning process;
- encourage student creativity;
- develop leadership;
- foster an informal, relaxed atmosphere for learning.

The **materials**
- offer clear objectives for each course and session;
- provide suggestions for evaluating student progress toward the objectives;

- include supplementary teaching helps such as posters and pictures;
- offer elements for use in the family to coordinate the teaching of knowledge and attitudes;
- use artwork, photographs, and print size suitable for each age level.

Using Materials Properly

Help your teachers use their materials properly. Remind them that they have a bigger task than merely transmitting facts. They teach students.

Of course, this teaching *must include the transmission of Bible truths*. But the goal must be *spiritual growth of the students* in their Christian understanding, attitudes, skills, and actions. Teachers must not teach materials for their own sake. Rather, they seek the spiritual growth of God's people.

Therefore, teachers must feel free to adapt the materials to their own style and to their students' needs and interests. Of course, the Bible is always relevant. But students need to learn that these scriptural truths are relevant to them. Teachers need to know their students. Then Sunday morning activities can apply Bible truths to the everyday lives, hopes, and aspirations of those students.

Help your teachers use their resources well. Have them go through the materials at the beginning of each quarter to identify the objectives and subject matter for each session. Encourage teachers to think about their lessons often. Perhaps reading material or experiences will uncover special lesson applications.

Also, encourage teachers to observe their students' everyday lives. These may reveal additional application ideas. Help teachers think creatively of ways to illustrate and apply the Bible truths in the lessons.

Stewardship and Mission Education

A Sunday school experience should prepare and equip God's people to function as Christian citizens in society and as responsible members of their church.

Stewardship education leads students to be more aware of their responsibility to care for the resources of God's creation and to utilize them for human good. God created people to be the managers of His creation. God has given us all we are and possess. He wills that we use them in ways that glorify Him and bring blessings to other people.

Through stewardship education students can learn ways to identify and develop their talents. Students also learn how to manage their time. How do they use time for personal enrichment, family life, recreation, study, work, meditation, worship, and service to others? Also, how do they manage their money and other possessions? God has given them these gifts not only for personal enjoyment and enrichment, but also for the material and spiritual welfare of others.

Usually the Christian is a member of a family. Each family member has responsibilities toward the others in the home. Church and community activities are important, but so is the family. Do all you can to help support your teachers' and students' family lives.

We also live in community with other human beings. God gives us a responsibility to do good to all people. We usually begin with those closest to us.

In the beginning God created human beings to take care of His creation. This includes environmental education. Stewardship education includes leading people to recognize their responsibility to other people and assisting them in fulfilling it.

Through our baptism the Holy Spirit placed us also in a community of believers, a congregation. God has given us various talents and gifts. He gives them so we can share them, especially with other members of our church. Help students identify the blessings God has given them. How can they be used to build up the members of the congregation? Then provide opportunities for students to use these blessings for the common good.

Your lesson materials will offer frequent opportunities for stewardship education. In addition, look for projects through which your students can use their blessings for their church or community.

Include personal counseling in your stewardship education. Help children and youth learn to know their capabilities and limitations. Show how these affect their life occupations.

Also provide guidance as students select a course of higher education. Students might also develop their talents through volunteer work and other helpful activities. For example, some students are qualified to enter one of the church's professions. Urge them to consider this opportunity for service. Also provide such persons with service opportunities within your congregation. This can help them assess their aptitude for such work and develop those talents and skills needed for the church's ministry. Encourage these students to pursue a course of study that will provide a foundation for later college and seminary studies.

One can hardly overemphasize the importance of mission education. Your congregation has freely chosen to associate itself with other congregations that profess the same faith as yours. Through this larger association of congregations, or denomination, you

- help prepare ministers of the church;
- provide Christian education materials and services;
- establish new congregations in your own and other countries;
- sustain small, struggling groups of Christians;
- maintain a wider ministry with youth;
- provide services to people in need;
- participate in many other ministries that your congregation could not accomplish by itself.

Through your Sunday school you can help the students identify with their denomination and its ministry. They need to learn its teachings, its history, its customs, its way of worship, and its various activities in their behalf. They need to develop a positive attitude toward their church and a desire to be part of its worldwide ministry.

The curriculum materials will offer many opportunities for you and the teachers to stimulate interest in, and support for, mission work. Your denomination may provide the following opportunities for mission education:

- Videotapes of movies about your church's mission activities.
- Missionaries or other persons from outside the congregation who can address the students about their work and about the church at large.
- Periodicals and books for information and inspiration.
- Mission projects. Select a specific field of work and write for information about that area. Give students an opportunity learn what your church body is doing and to bring gifts for the work in that particular field.

For most people the Sunday school is the primary agency through which they will be instructed in the Christian faith and life. You have many opportunities for ministry. Your Sunday school deserves and needs your best leadership and guidance as it plans a full program for the Christian education of its adults, youth, and children.

Questions for Discussion

1. How well do your study materials meet the needs of your Sunday school? (See "Evaluating Religious Curricular Materials and Resources" listed at the end of this book.) What supplementary materials and activities might you plan to increase the effectiveness of your study materials?

2. What criteria do you use in selecting curricular materials? How do these criteria compare with those mentioned in this chapter?

3. What training experiences do you currently offer new teachers? experienced teachers? How might you strengthen your teacher training program?

4. What audiovisual equipment and materials does your Sunday school have? How do you catalog your holdings? What arrangements have you made for the care of your AV equipment and resources? How might these arrangements be improved?

5. What does your Sunday school do to help teachers and students develop their sense of stewardship? What else might you do?

6. What program of mission education does your Sunday school have?

5 Your Ministry in the Congregation

As a Sunday school leader, look for ways to show interest in the spiritual growth of all members of your congregation. Children in your Sunday school need the support and Christian nurture of their parents. They also need the encouragement and example of older youth and adults of the congregation.

Youth and adults also need opportunities for systematic study of the Scriptures. Such study can equip them to function as people of God in church and society.

Ministries with Families
Nursery Roll

In Baptism the person is baptized into the community of God's people. Parents have the primary responsibility for the new Christian's growth in faith. However, your congregation also has a responsibility to this new member.

You can use a nursery-roll program to support the parents and at the same time fulfill part of your obligation toward the child. To begin, appoint a nursery (cradle) roll coordinator to manage this ministry to the very young children and parents.

The nursery-roll coordinator assists through a planned program of mailings and home visits. A nursery-roll packet available from Concordia Publishing House contains materials to share with parents.

Be sure to include home visits in your nursery-roll program. If necessary, find and train volunteers to assist the nursery-roll coordinator.

The first visit to the home of an infant might occur shortly after birth. Or plan this first visit shortly after the child's baptism. Then plan at least one additional visit each year until the child is enrolled in a Sunday school class.

Involve your pastor in the selection and training of personnel for your nursery-roll program. This ministry can be a great blessing to children, parents, and your entire congregation.

Classes for Parents and Children

Classes for two-year-olds and their parents offer tremendous potential for ministry with families.

As teachers interact with young children, parents also are involved in the educational process. Also, discussion with and among parents can help them plan ways to train their children. Both kinds of activities equip parents to reinforce the Sunday school experiences. In this way they remain their children's primary teachers.

See the Concordia Publishing House catalog for additional information about instructional materials for parents and 2's.

Ministry Through Mail

Attempt to develop an ongoing ministry to parents by means of mail. When a new student enrolls, send a letter to welcome the child. Also inform the parents about the purposes and procedures of the school.

Perhaps you can develop a Sunday school handbook. An overview of your purposes and procedures can help both parents and the Sunday school staff. You might include the handbook in this letter of welcome.

Some Sunday schools publish a newsletter. In some instances this newsletter is prepared entirely by staff members. In other cases students contribute to the letter and thus make it their own publication. If your school does not have a newsletter, send occasional mailings to parents to keep them advised of your Sunday school's progress and activities.

Consider sending greeting cards to students on birthday or Baptism anniversaries. You might also send cards to students who have been absent or ill. See the Concordia Publishing House catalog for cards especially designed for such occasions.

In a few instances persons unable to attend Sunday school desire to be served by mail. Look for ways to give the regular Sunday school materials to these people. At the beginning of each quarter a person from the Sunday school staff, possibly the pastor, might visit the home of these people. In cases of great distances you will need to use the mail and telephone for most communication.

Ministry through Meetings

You might arrange occasional meetings with parents. Involve them in the Sunday school's ministry and support them in their parental roles.

Possibly set one meeting at the beginning of each Sunday school year. Invite both parents and staff. Discuss the purposes of the school and accept suggestions for improving the school. Teachers and parents might work together to set Sunday school goals for the coming year. Share pertinent information, but also be sure to get reactions and ideas from the parents.

Additional meetings with parents might be held throughout the year. Select topics that interest the parents and provide a program that will support and equip participants to be Christian parents—often under difficult circumstances.

Following are some topics that might be helpful to parents:

- How to conduct home devotions.
- How to assist children in Bible study and lesson preparation.
- How to nurture spiritual growth of children.
- How to deal with problems that parents face.
- How to communicate with children.

As you schedule meetings, be aware of home situations in your congregation (e.g., one-parent households).

Ministry through Visits

Home visitations can make valuable contributions to a Sunday school ministry. Can your teachers make visits in homes of newly enrolled students? During these visits they can learn to know the students and parents better. This will prepare teachers to apply lesson materials to the lives of students. Also, this initial contact can do much to build goodwill with parents.

Continued visits in the homes will help teachers better understand the backgrounds of their students. Ideally, teachers will call on absentees promptly.

Some teachers may be able to visit homes quarterly. During these visits they can deliver and give an overview of materials to be used during the next quarter. Such visits can help maintain good relations with students and parents. Some parents may use this opportunity to enlist the aid of the teacher in helping students with their problems.

Other Ministry Opportunities

You might plan social events for parents and their children. These can cultivate parental involvement in the Sunday school while also meeting needs of parents and their children. Parent-children banquets or dinners, picnics, and group attendance at sports and other events are but a few possibilities.

Encourage parents to visit Sunday school occasionally. For example, invite mothers to visit their children's classes on Mother's Day, and invite fathers on Father's Day. At such times be sure to be sensitive to those children in special circumstances, such as living with one parent.

Consider Sunday school classes for parents. This setting serves parents as well as their children with a Christian education ministry. It also gives opportunities to involve parents in the overall Sunday school program. Plan ways to help parents develop skills in

- family worship;
- child care and discipline;
- listening and communication;
- other areas of parenting.

During these classes parents can meet other moms and dads and compare notes.

Some parent classes study the Scripture text used for their children's study materials. Thereby parents are better able to discuss with their children their lesson at home.

Ministry with the Entire Congregation

Building Sunday School Participation

Worship Services

The worship service is an important educational setting. The order of service, as well as the sensitive, thoughtful sermon, offers many opportunities for learning.

Small Groups

But worship services have limitations. Some subjects are better discussed in small groups. Here members can express disagreements, raise questions, and share views and experiences. Small groups give participants opportunities to explore biblical books and themes in depth and over a period of time.

Bible Study

Your parish has a responsibility to provide all its members with opportunities for Bible study. Involve members in the selection of subject matter so that real needs are met. Classes may study a book of the Bible or a topic of interest. The nature of the group and the topic will help you determine the length of each offering. Most congregations offer courses that last 4–13 weeks. See the Concordia Publishing House catalog for a list of courses available.

Plan your youth and adult educational program for a period of time, perhaps a quarter or semester. Then widely publicize the topics, the names of the leaders, and the meeting places and times. Arrange for a convenient place for preregistration of participants, such as in the narthex of the church. Invite people in person, or at least by telephone, to join the group of their choice.

Youth and adult classes that meet identifiable needs, have competent leaders, are well planned and publicized, and enlist students by direct invitation have a good chance at success.

"Unified Services"

Some church members complain, "I don't have enough time." Such youth and adults often stay away from Sunday Bible study. Also, their children may not attend worship services.

Such excuses have little or no validity. Nevertheless, some churches meet this objection by offering a "unified service" in addition to the regular service. A unified service may take the place of a Sunday school's opening assembly. The pastor leads this worship. He plans a service appropriate for all members of the family.

After the service participants go directly to their study groups. Some congregation thereby compress the entire Sunday worship and study experience into 90 or 100 minutes.

This plan brings all age groups the the church setting both for worship and for study. Congregations who follow this plan also provide a second service for those who prefer a more traditional worship setting.

Informing the Congregation

The Sunday school belongs to the entire congregation. All members ought to be interested in maintaining a vibrant school. But members need to be informed.

Most congregations select a board of education to oversee and strengthen the congregation's educational agencies. Usually the superintendent is responsible to this board and is to be closely involved in its work. A superintendent can

- provide this board with periodic reports on the Sunday school's work;
- advise the board of the school's needs;
- encourage board members to take an active interest in all phases of Sunday school activity.

Through the board of education the superintendent makes regular reports to the voters' assembly. This is a fine opportunity to broaden the congregation's vision for its Sunday school. The superintendent maintains an overall positive tone in the regular reports but does not ignore problems that need to be resolved or challenges that must be met.

Gaining Congregational Support

In addition to official reports, you can use a variety of avenues for increasing the congregation's support for its Sunday school and teachers.

Observe Christian Education Month, probably in September.

During September, members of your church are already thinking about education. This provides a natural time for a Christian education emphasis.

During late spring or early summer your congregation probably receives a packet of resources for Christian Education Month. This packet will likely include sample Rally Day service forms, tracts, Christian Education Month observance suggestions, and other helpful items. Examine the materials thoroughly and make good use of them.

Observe Rally Day, or Christian Education Sunday on one Sunday during September.

During this service the Sunday school staff might be placed in their offices. Encourage your pastor to highlight their vital role in Christian growth. Sunday school students may participate in this service in prominent and meaningful ways.

Hold a Sunday school open house on a Sunday morning and on a weekday evening. Give congregation members a firsthand view of your activities. You might also display some work done by students.

Sponsor a recognition dinner for Sunday school workers.

Throughout the year keep your congregational members aware of their Sunday school. Publicize the school in Sunday bulletins and parish newsletters. Display the work of students on bulletin boards. Involve Sunday school students in services and programs. Ask your pastor to mention the Sunday school's efforts whenever appropriate occasions arise.

Work to involve all members of the parish—adults and youth as well as children—in your Sunday school program. Such efforts can strengthen your program and help you more effectively provide Christian education for God's people.

Questions for Discussion

1. Does your Sunday school have a nursery (cradle) roll? If not, why and how will you begin one? If you have a program, who is responsible? What does this person or team do? How might the nursery roll in your congregation be improved?

2. What mailings do you now send parents of Sunday school students? What future mailings might you plan?

3. What kind of visitation program does your Sunday school now have? How might it be expanded?

4. What value do you see in meeting with parents? What parent meetings does your Sunday school sponsor? What else might you do to further involve parents in Sunday school life?

5. What youth, adult, and parent study groups does your Sunday school have? What kinds of study groups might your Sunday school organize in the future?

6. What did your Sunday school do during your last Christian Education Month? What might it do next September? What ongoing program of public relations within your congregation might you set up or expand?

6 You and Your Community

A basic reason for our existence on earth as Christians is that we by word and example might give witness to the world of the grace of God in Jesus Christ. God redeemed us by the saving work of Christ and called us into His family by the operation of the Holy Spirit. He has also chosen to reveal Himself to other people through us.

This suggests a primary purpose of your Sunday school: *To reach out to the people in your community and to share with them the saving love of Jesus.* In leading the unchurched in your community to Christ, you also lead them into your fellowship. Then they, in turn, may participate in the mission of God's church.

Public Relations

We reach out in a number of ways. One group of activities are commonly called "public relations." These affect the image of your congregation—and of the Gospel of Jesus Christ—in your community. Public relations include everything your church and its members do to make some kind of impression on the people about you. These activities lead them to form attitudes about your church and the message you proclaim.

Facilities

Your physical plant's appearance influences attitudes of those around you. Unkempt and unattractive facilities could lead passersby to think the people of your parish do not really care about your church or the Gospel it teaches. On the other hand, neat and tidy classrooms not only makes the Sunday school a cheerful place for students, but also demonstrates that you care about what you are doing.

Program

"Public relations" includes a well-organized, smoothly functioning Sunday school program. Not only does it contribute to the Sunday school's effectiveness; it can also lead a casual visitor to want to return. Moreover, word of mouth may spread the news about a good Sunday school. This, too, makes the school more attractive to potential visitors and members.

Students and Teachers

Your Sunday school members and the quality of their lives also play a significant role in the image your school projects. As the students grow in Christian attitudes and behavior, their lives become a powerful witness to the grace of God and what it can accomplish in human beings.

Students reflect in their community the quality of their home life and their Sunday school experiences. Ideally students will demonstrate that

- they know what they believe;
- they are committed to the Christian faith;
- they seek to live in Christian love as the fruit of their faith.

Your school is involved in public relations merely by existing. But planned projects that you sponsor can help project a positive image in your Sunday school.

Newspapers

Take an inventory of the public media available to you. Then plan how you can use them to inform your area of your school and its ministry. Community newspapers usually welcome well-written news items from churches in the area they serve. Identify a member of your congregation who writes well. Ask and help this person prepare articles about your Sunday school activities and submit them to local newspapers.

You can cultivate the goodwill of community newspapers and also publicize your school through occasional advertisements. Some schools use paid advertisements to present a Christian message and invite unchurched people to their Sunday school. Paid advertisements might also publicize events to which the public is invited, such as Rally Day or the children's Christmas service. Many community newspapers will add news coverage when churches purchase advertising.

Radio

Look for ways to use radio stations in your area. They may be happy to broadcast items about your Sunday school as a public service. Some stations broadcast lists of community events. Provide them with notices of your Sunday school activities. Consider radio spot announcements to give a Christian message and invite people to your school.

Your school might even prepare and present an entire program on radio. Some stations will present a 15- or 30-minute Sunday school session with child participation. Or your children might present a program of Christian music, especially at such seasons as Christmas, Lent, and Easter.

Television

Expect more work when you use television. Nevertheless, you might explore the possibilities available. Many cable television companies offer time to churches and other local groups. If you plan to use this time, look for technical guidance. A poor program may be worse than none at all. However, a good offering can make a significant impact in your community.

Also look for ways to publicize television programs offered by your denomination. Consider announcements or advertising in newspapers and on radio stations.

Displays

Some merchants are willing to give window space in their stores to community organizations. You might display posters advertising such events as Rally Day, Sunday school presentations, or the vacation Bible school. Merchants may be more willing to display posters made by children than those purchased from a commercial source.

Community events offer opportunities to draw attention to your Sunday school. Your school might prepare and manage a booth at a fair. Or, if your community is planning a parade, your school might enter a float.

You may not see immediate results from any one public relations project. Effects tend to be cumulative. As people hear more and more about your Sunday school through newspapers, radio, public displays, and community events, they will become more and more conscious of your school. Perhaps some will want to become a part of it.

Personal Community Outreach

Do not stop with public-relations activities. Also look for ways to reach out to the unchurched in your community in direct, person-to-person ways. Through personal outreach and witness you fulfill a significant part of your mission to the world.

Training for Outreach

Sunday school teachers regularly speak of their faith to their students. Help them speak also to unchurched friends and acquaintances. Some teachers feel inadequate to share their faith with nonbelievers. Training can help them overcome those feelings and become more effective witnesses.

Also help your teachers equip their students to become evangelists for Christ. Students have many opportunities to speak of their faith and their Sunday school. But they may be afraid to talk about Christ; they may fear ridicule or rejection by their friends. They need to learn how to share the Gospel in a gracious, winsome way.

Now, the Good News, a Concordia Sunday School Teacher Education course, has been designed for situations such as these. You may use this course to equip teachers both to be witnesses for Jesus themselves and to help their students develop skills in speaking of Jesus to others. Encourage all Sunday school workers to take this course.

Opportunities for Outreach

Outreach occurs most naturally when God's people speak of their faith as opportunities arise in conversations with family, friends, and neighbors. Many Sunday schools grow because teachers, parents, and students talk enthusiastically about their school.

Children might also distribute attractive handbills or doorknob hangers in the church's neighborhood. These materials might briefly describe the message of the church and offer a friendly invitation to visit.

Community Canvasses

Ideally, a congregation will visit every home in its community to identify unchurched people, to speak to them about Jesus, and to invite them to worship services and Sunday school.

Some churches canvass 20 percent of their neighborhood each year. After five years the canvass is complete and the rotation begins again.

As you organize these visitations, be sure the canvassers get the names of the children as well as the parents in homes of unchurched families. Then plan follow-up visits to cultivate interest in your church and Sunday school. Each follow-up visit should be made in a friendly, inviting tone. Being gracious can help keep the door open for future visits.

Bus Ministries

In some communities bus ministries can be very effective. Through this ministry you may be able to reach many children who would not otherwise attend your classes or worship.

You might connect bus ministry with your community canvass. Send periodic mailings to families who have shown any kind of interest in your congregation. Include the schedule for the Sunday school bus.

Be sure to train your bus drivers in ways to witness as they interact with children and their families. If possible, arrange for one or more other adults to assist the drivers in this ministry.

Reaching New Residents

New residents in your community are potential members of your Sunday school. You may be able to get the names and addresses of new residents from a utility company or from another source.

Regularly train members of your congregation to be alert to new neighbors and to invite them along to your church and Sunday school. Most new residents are seeking to become acquainted in their surroundings. They may welcome invitations to a church if these are made in a warm, friendly spirit.

Activities at Sites Away from the Church

You can extend your Sunday school through retreats, camping experiences, and other Christian education events away from the church plant. Some people who will not come to your church immediately may participate in an event held away from church.

Some of your members might organize backyard Bible clubs. These members would open their homes to neighborhood children for Bible study and sociability.

Club meetings may be held in a backyard, on a porch, or at a similar gathering place within the community served by your Sunday school. Invite children by written invitation or word-of-mouth.

Sessions may last one or more hours. Tell Bible and mission stories, teach songs, and pray with the children. Puppets, games, action songs, and refreshments may be elements of the program.

A club may meet one or more days during the week. In spring and fall it may meet after school or on Saturday, but during the summer the club could meet for five days during the week (Monday through Friday) and use the Concordia vacation Bible school program.

Other Outreach Programs

Tel-a-Friend. This outreach method utilizes the desire of most children to talk to other children over the telephone. Children can listen to recorded messages by calling a local telephone number. For more information see the *Evangelism for Sunday School Growth* booklet listed in the resources section at the end of this guide.

Coordination with other programs. Extend the outreach of your Sunday school by coordinating your effort with those of summer programs or weekday schools of religion. Some children begin to attend Sunday school after participation in those activities. Look for ways to invite neighborhood children to attend a vacation Bible school, a summer camp, or a weekday program held after school hours.

Come, Grow with Us. This resource is designed to help your Sunday school develop or strengthen its outreach program. See the Concordia Publishing House catalog for ordering information.

As a leader of your Sunday school, you have many significant opportunities to serve the people of your parish and the residents of your community. Your ministry of fostering spiritual growth is well worth your best efforts. What joy must be yours as you recognize your opportunities for service and realize that the Spirit of God Himself is present to bless your endeavors!

Questions for Discussion

1. Who is responsible for the upkeep of your Sunday school facilities? What improvements, if any, should take place in the care of your facilities?

2. Do the teachers in your Sunday school strive to develop Christian attitudes and actions as well as knowledge? How can a proper understanding of the Gospel contribute to a person's relationships with other people?

3. What newspapers in your community are available for your Sunday school's news items and advertisements? What use do you make of them to publicize your school? How might you use your community newspapers more effectively?

4. What are you doing to help your teachers develop skills in outreach? To help your students? What else might you do?

5. When did your church last canvass your community to identify unchurched families? What plans do you have for the future? What might you do to make your church more sensitive to the unchurched in your neighborhood?

6. What outreach programs does your Sunday school now have? What might your Sunday school do in outreach during the next 12 months?

Resource Materials

The following items may be ordered from Concordia Publishing House, 3558 South Jefferson Avenue, Saint Louis, MO 63118.

Building and Equipment, S08342.

Bus Ministry (evangelism resource book 9), 09-2393.

Caring for Infants and Toddlers, S08423.

Creative Environments for Christian Education, S08186.

Evangelism for Sunday School Growth, S08264.

Family Life Education in Your Congregation, S08377.

How Is Our Sunday School Doing? (An evaluation instrument), S08620.

In Ministry: Parents with Children Birth to Three, S08603.

Instrument for Evaluating Religious Curricular Materials and Resources, S08477.

Organizing and Maintaining the Sunday School, S08255.

Over 200 Ways to Improve Sunday School, 12-2811.

Parent Education in Your Congregation, S08158.

Planning for Lutheran Early Childhood Programs, S08325.

Resources (an annual publication listing resources produced by the Board for Parish Services of The Lutheran Church—Missouri Synod), S08469.

Sunday School Teacher Selection, Training and Support, S08359.

Teaching Disabled Students in the Sunday School, S08530.

The Small Sunday School, S08257.

Appendix A

Evaluating Religious Curricular Materials and Resources

Select a piece of curricular material you wish to evaluate. Follow the steps listed in this appendix. Then make your final recommendation about the use and usefulness of the material.

Course Title: _____
Publisher: _____

Step 1: Read the title of the course, the table of contents, and the introduction (preface, foreword).

a. What is the content of this course? (What is it about?)
b. Who is the course for? (Who can use it?)
c. What is the purpose of the course? (What is it intended to accomplish for the person who uses it?)
d. Will the content and the purpose of this course fit the needs of the learners in your parish? (Will it touch their lives? What will be the specific value of this course for your learners?)
e. Do the content and purpose of this course fit the spiritual and educational goals you have for your parish?

STOP now if you have answered no to either of the last two questions. The materials you are looking at are not right for your purposes.

Step 2: Read a lesson. Read both the learners materials and teachers guide. Make notes as you read. Then answer the following questions. Don't just answer the questions yes/no. Write down what prompts you to answer as you do.

Theological Adequacy

1. Regardless of its purpose, a lesson must **focus** on God and His acting toward His people. Any material that centers on people—any material that seems to feature the doings of people or to use people as mere examples of how we are to act—is out of focus. How is this lesson **focused on God** and His acts toward us (on our behalf)?
2. A lesson tells the **truth.** It must be accurate in its presentation of Scripture and it must treat Scripture truthfully and faithfully. Is this lesson **true to Scripture?**
3. **LAW:** Every time we come into contact with God's Word, it reveals His will (Law). We are accused because we fail to keep that law. How does the lesson **confront** the learner with the will of God? How does that encounter with God's will do more than tell the learner what he or she should be doing or should not be doing? How does it move the learner to realize that he or she is in need of forgiveness in Jesus Christ?
4. **GOSPEL:** How does the lesson comfort the learner with the Good News of God's unconditional love (forgiveness) in Jesus Christ? How does it proclaim the Gospel—apply the Gospel to the needs of the learner?
5. As a result of an encounter with the Word—especially the Good News of salvation in Jesus Christ—the people are changed. By the work of the Spirit their faith is strengthened, their sins are forgiven, their spirits are renewed, and they are empowered to want to live according to God's will. That change is not a mere decision to live better lives. It is a change accomplished by the Spirit. What is this lesson moving people to do or to be? How does the motivation and power for change lie in the Spirit—and not in the earnest strivings of the Christian to accomplish his or her own righteousness?
6. Not only must the Gospel be clearly proclaimed; it must predominate. How does the Gospel lie at the heart of this lesson and shape the overall effect of the lesson for the learner?

STOP now if the materials you are evaluating have not passed the questions of theological adequacy. If the materials are not faithful to Scripture, if they do not focus on God's gracious acts of salvation, if they confuse Law and Gospel—they are not acceptable as religious education resources and may, in fact, actually do great harm to the faith-life of the people who use them.

Educational Design

1. Is the lesson **interesting?** Does it intersect the interests of the learner? Why or why not?
2. **Level:** Is the lesson written so that the people for whom it is prepared can understand it? Is it too difficult? too easy?
3. Are the educational **methods** and activities varied? involving? useful? Are they appropriate to the age level of your class?
4. Does the lesson have **integrity?** Does it all hang together, move in a single direction, make a single point? Is it clear, easy to follow and present?
5. **Cognitive/Affective Balance:** Does the lesson touch the emotions (feelings) as well as the mind? Do the objectives of the lesson move toward goals for heart as well as head, for doing as well as knowing?

Graphic Design

1. Is the material attractive? Is the **artwork** helpful and appealing to the learner?
2. Do the **layout and design** of the lesson assist learning?

Teachers Materials

1. Are the teachers materials **clear,** helpful, and detailed enough to assist a new teacher?
2. Are there enough **options** to help both the new and experienced teacher adapt this material to his or her class?
3. Does the teachers guide list and provide adequate **resources?**
4. Are the statements of purpose, of **goals,** of objectives clear and helpful?
5. Do the **activities** fit (support, reinforce) the goals and objectives for the lesson?
6. Will the teacher going into a class feel well equipped using these materials? If not, why not?

Step 3: Repeat the procedure from step 2 with another lesson. Look over your notes. Then answer the following questions. **If you cannot answer yes to all, the material is not right for your purposes.**

a. Does this course "fit" the needs and interests of the people in your parish?
b. Is this course true to Scripture and your church body's teachings, based on the Bible, and centered in Jesus Christ?

c. Is this course effective as a learning tool for participants and as a teaching tool for the leader?
d. Will those who use this course grow in their knowledge of Scripture, their faith in Jesus, and/or their ability to live their faith?

Recommendations for this material:

_____
_____
_____
_____
_____
_____
_____
_____
_____
_____
_____
_____
_____
_____
_____
_____
_____
_____

Adapted from *Instrument for Evaluating Religious Curricular Materials and Resources,* Board for Parish Services Information Bulletin #90886.

Appendix B

Annual Planning Guide for Superintendents
ORGANIZING CLASSES

Parents and Twos

Teacher(s) _____
Location(s) _____
Classroom Supplies _____

Material to Order Quarterly _____
_____

Ages 3–4

Teacher(s) _____
Location(s) _____
Classroom Supplies _____

Material to Order Quarterly _____
_____

Kindergarten

Teacher(s) _____
Location(s) _____
Classroom Supplies _____

Material to Order Quarterly _____
_____

Grades 1–2

Teacher(s) _____
Location(s) _____
Classroom Supplies _____

Material to Order Quarterly _____
_____

Grades 3–4

Teacher(s) _____
Location(s) _____
Classroom Supplies_____
_____
Material to Order Quarterly _____
_____

Grades 5–6

Teacher(s) _____
Location(s) _____
Classroom Supplies_____
_____
Material to Order Quarterly _____
_____

Grades 7–8

Teacher(s) _____
Location(s) _____
Classroom Supplies_____
_____
Material to Order Quarterly _____
_____

Special Education

Teacher(s) _____
Location(s) _____
Classroom Supplies_____
_____
Material to Order Quarterly _____
_____

High School

Teacher(s) _____
Location(s) _____
Classroom Supplies_____
_____
Material to Order Quarterly _____
_____

Adult

Teacher(s) _____
Location(s) _____
Classroom Supplies _____

Material to Order Quarterly _____

Additional Staff

Substitute Teachers _____
Song or Worship Leaders _____
Classroom Helpers _____

Equipment and Supplies

Audio/Visual _____
Arts and Crafts _____

Other: _____

Other Needs

Work Area _____
Storage Area _____
Helpers _____
Attendance Forms _____
Supplies for Awards _____

Plans for the Year

Schedule of Staff Meetings _____
Teacher Education Plans _____
Sunday School Publicity Plans _____
Schedule of Special Events _____
Plan for Follow-up Visits or Mailings to Absentees _____
Plan for Introductory Visits to New Members _____
Plan for Public Recognition of Sunday School Staff _____

Other: _____

Other: _____

Appendix C

Weekly Checklist for Superintendents

Before Classes Begin

____ Teaching areas are in order
____ Tables in place (correct number and height)
____ Chairs in place (correct number and size)
____ Equipment and supplies provided
____ Lights turned on
____ Heat or air conditioning turned on
____ Dividers in place

____ Other: _____

____ Teachers and helpers are present
____ Substitutes if needed are present and necessary instructions have been given to them
____ Arrangements have been made for special activities

____ Other: _____

During Class Sessions

____ Visitors are welcomed to Sunday school office: information about them is recorded and they are brought to their classes
____ Attendance reports are received
____ Attendance is properly recorded
____ Visitor cards are distributed; follow-up procedures are begun
____ Procedures are begun to follow-up on absentees
____ Offering money is received and recorded; money has been given to appropriate person for deposit

____ Other: _____

After Class Sessions

___ Friendly farewells are given
___ Visitors are invited to return
___ All students have departed; especially the young children have been met by family members of others so designated by their families
___ Thanks is expressed to teachers and helpers
___ Rooms are placed in order for other church activities
___ Lights are turned off
___ Heat or air conditioning is adjusted, if necessary
___ Custodian has been notified of special needs

___ Other: _____

___ Other: _____

___ Other: _____